Side by Side

Side by Side

Team-Building Devotions for the
Gospel-Centered Workplace

Cynthia Hopkins

Bold Vision Books
PO Box 2011
Friendswood, Texas 77549

ISBN 9781946708120
LCCN 2017-951297

Cover Art by © Ryhor Bruyeu | Dreamstime.com
Cover Design by Maddie Scott

Published in the Unites States of America

Bold Vision Books
PO Box 2011
Friendswood, Texas 77549

Dedication

To the hours 9 to 5
and all the people who want them to
mean something bigger.

Table of Contents

Introduction
&
How to Use This Book

As a freelance writer for the better part of two decades, I've had the great privilege of authoring and co-authoring many gospel-centered projects. Most of the time, that happens because editors have assigned specific writing assignments. Some of those projects are attached to the works of other authors, pastors, and teachers. Some are meant to minister to teenagers, women, parents, or senior adults. In most, my part is largely anonymous. But no matter the Bible study, article, or devotion's target audience, and no matter how great or small its distribution, I always find myself immensely grateful for the opportunity to invest in the body of Christ.

Side by Side is special to me for that reason and more. This project is a direct result of the vision of a Christian camp director for his employees. Dear friends Kim and Jaroy Carpenter work at Lakeview Camp and Retreat Center, south of the Dallas-Fort Worth metroplex. Compelled by a desire to invest in the spiritual growth of the camp staff as well as form meaningful connections, Jaroy asked me to write weekly devotions department directors could lead with their teams. I wrote those devotions specifically with

9

the camp's vision statement in mind, and with a healthy knowledge of the particular needs of the Lakeview staff.

My publisher friends George and Karen Porter at Bold Vision Books thought other gospel-centered organizations could benefit from the devotions as a resource for their own teams. What you hold in your hands is those original devotions revised so any camp, church, or business can connect weekly in fellowship, Bible study, and prayer.

The book is structured with 48 weeks of devotions and 4 weeks of "bonus" material. The 48 weeks are sequential. The four bonus devotions are meant to be used at your discretion on holiday weeks and at other times to round out the 52-week year.

Each devotion begins with an icebreaker question. The *Icebreaker*, *Scripture*, and *Ask all* sections can be read directly to your group. The talking points in the other sections are intended to help form the basis of your leader-introduced discussion. These devotions will work best when you allow the Scripture and bullet points to serve as springboards to launch your group where it needs to go. Let discussion flow naturally.

The team at Bold Vision Books, Lakeview Camp and Retreat Center, and I are praying for God to use these devotions for His great glory and the good of your organization beyond what we can imagine. As He does, we'd love to hear about it. Would you do us the honor of sharing your stories with us? Email us at sidebysidedevotions@ gmail.com.

Blessings,
Cynthia

Week 1

Testimony

Icebreaker:

Show or read your organization's mission statement. Ask, "How is this true? Are we carrying out our mission?" If you don't have one, ask, "If we had a mission statement, what do you think it should be? Why?"

Segue:

What happens in and among each one of us is the first step in the process of carrying out the mission of this organization. We're not just spectators. We're not just along for the ride or even to complete a list of tasks each day (name whatever your team's responsibilities include.) It would be a terrible waste if we didn't also have the hope and expectation for God to use our time here to move in us to affect change in the world beyond this place.

Ask all:

When did you first come to faith in Christ?

Scripture: Read Revelation 12:11.

11

Connect & Discuss:

▶ When we use the word testimony, we tend to think about our personal stories. But that's not how it's used in this verse. We all have different stories, but in Christ, we share the same testimony – Jesus is Savior and Lord.

▶ It's His blood on the cross, and the position we allow Him to take in our lives that causes us to overcome, nothing else.

▶ So whether your past was terrible or your life has been mostly smooth sailing, whether you grew up in church or didn't, it doesn't matter. We're all on equal footing before Jesus. And this workplace is a part of your faith story now. Whether you realize it or not, God is actively at work in you, right here, right now as an employee of _____. He's not interested in any of us merely earning a paycheck. His plans are much bigger than that.

Challenge:

In Christ, you overcome the world. In Christ, you get to take part in changing it, too. Will you let Him show you how?

Pray

Week 2

Currently Craving...

Icebreaker:

What is one thing you know how to do better now than you did when you first started working here? What would (name of organization or business) be like if we all acted like it was still our first day at work?

Segue:

When you start a new job, you have to learn how to do things. You don't know exactly what your boss expects. Hopefully, over time, you learn. A person without a teachable spirit, an employee who doesn't care to improve, probably won't. Relationship with Christ is a learning and growing process, too. The changes that take place in us happen over time, but how much we desire and pursue growth affects how quickly it happens.

Ask all:

How would you describe your relationship with Christ, currently? Stagnant or growing? Why?

Scripture: Read 1 Peter 2:2-3.

Connect & Discuss:

▶ Spiritual maturity isn't something that just happens to us. We have responsibility in it. These verses indicate there's a natural response when we experience salvation in Christ ("since you have tasted the Lord is good"): we will long to know and apply spiritual truths to our lives. Peter said we have to crave it.

▶ Ask, "What's a food you crave? How far would you go/have you gone to get it? What would it look like for you to crave spiritual change and growth? What is one area of spiritual change or growth you would like to see in your life?

Challenge:

If you're a believer, you've experienced (tasted) the goodness of Jesus. No matter how old you are or how long you've been a Christian, there's more! How much of Him you experience this week is up to you.

Pray

Week 3

You Can Have It All

Icebreaker:

Which do you consider a more important quality in a coworker? A wealth of knowledge or a good attitude? Happiness or a strong work ethic? A sense of humor or trustworthiness?

Segue:

It's hard to choose one good quality over another. Most of us like to find them all in the people we work with. You wouldn't accept dishonesty in a person if they explained, "That's just the way I am." You would expect that person to start working on being more honest, right?

Ask all:

Name a character trait or fruit of the Spirit (from Galatians 5:22)—love, joy, peace, patience, kindness, goodness, gentleness, faithfulness, self-control—you'd like to be more evident in your life.

Scripture: Read 2 Peter 1:5-8.

Connect & Discuss:

▶ "This very reason" in verse 5 refers to verse 3 where Peter says God's power has given us everything we need to share in the divine nature and be godly people. In other words, in Christ, we are without excuse. As we follow Him, we continue to develop Christlike qualities every day of our lives.

▶ What characteristics does Peter name in verses 5-7? Peter says that if we don't have these qualities in *increasing* measure, our knowledge of Jesus is useless.

▶ In other words, we will never be the organization God intends us to be, impacting the world the way He wants us to, unless we're relying on God's power to walk in step with the Spirit.

Challenge:

Let's not settle for the qualities that come easiest to us. Don't resign yourself to your struggles, believing that's just the way you are. In Christ, that's not how you are. In Christ, you're filled with the power to increase in faith, goodness, knowledge, self-control, endurance, godliness, brotherly affection, and love; useful and fruitful in changing the world.

Pray

Week 4

Mind-bending Changes

Icebreaker:

Are you the type of person to go with the flow or against it? Is that a good thing or a bad thing? Explain.

Segue:

Scientists say a person's frontal lobe—the part of the brain that controls decision-making—doesn't fully develop until our mid-twenties. But guess what? It's not just the frontal lobe that needs to develop, and it's not just young adults who need it to happen. Our brains are hard-wired from birth to think selfish thoughts, worldly thoughts, wrong thoughts. So, in this sense, if you go with the flow of your natural way of thinking, you're headed the wrong way whether you're a teenage boy or an 82-year-old church-loving granny. Spiritually speaking, our minds should be in a constant state of transformation not just until we're 25, but throughout our entire lives.

Ask all:

What (or who) are some influences on the way you think?

Scripture: Read Romans 12:1-2.
Connect & Discuss:

▶ Paul pleaded to believers to give their bodies to God. Then he followed by speaking about one part of our bodies in particular – our minds. That's probably because our minds are the hardest body part for us to surrender.

▶ God's will is good and pleasing and perfect. The thing is, we can agree with that all we want; but we can't discern His good, pleasing, and perfect will unless we allow Him to renew our minds, bending our thoughts toward His.

▶ How are our minds renewed? By God's power, through His Word and the influence of the Holy Spirit. As that process takes place, we are changed. We stop going with the flow of our natural way of thinking and the world we live in, and are instead driven by the Truth He plants in us.

Challenge:

Lead everyone to say this: "I don't know everything." Now look at someone else and say, "But it's ok. None of us does." But if we'll commit to read and study God's Word and turn our frontal lobes and every other part of our brains over to the Holy Spirit, He'll lead us to truth. Think of it this way. God says what happens here (point to your head) needs to change you before you can change the world.

Pray

Week 5

Now You See Me

Icebreaker:

How do you unwind after a particularly rough day at work?

Segue:

Circumstances typically determine whether we judge a day as good or bad. You woke up late, had 34 voicemails and 47 emails waiting for you when you arrived, the hard drive on your computer crashed, your favorite coworker resigned, and your car battery died. That's a bad day.

You picked up Starbucks on the way to work and the cashier gave you a free muffin, you hit every green light, your boss was so impressed with your recent accomplishments that he took you to lunch and gave you a raise, and when you headed to your car at sunset, a nearby bird started singing what you're sure sounded exactly like Survivor's "Eye of the Tiger." That's a good day.

But what if there's more to "good" and "bad" than meets the eye?

Ask all:

Why are the visible circumstances of life a faulty place to put our focus?

Scripture: Read 2 Corinthians 4:16-18.

Connect & Discuss:

▶ In these verses, Paul contrasts here the outer self with the inner self, momentary light affliction with the incomparable eternal weight of glory. Think about that last phrase; it's a really big truth! He contrasts the unseen with the seen, and the temporary with the eternal.

▶ Think about it like this: some changes happen whether you acknowledge and invite them or not. You can have all the surgeries you want, but you can't stop the aging process. As your outer person is in a constant state of natural decline, your inner person is advancing toward eternity.

▶ That's why Paul says to change our ideas about good and bad from visible circumstances that don't last to the invisible truths wrapped up in God's plan that endures forever. God's purpose for us isn't earthly comfort and success. It's way bigger than that. Our "bad" days don't mean He doesn't love us; they mean this isn't our home. He has much to accomplish in and through us before we get there.

Challenge:

See God in the good and the bad. He's at work in both places.

Pray

Week 6

Increased Productivity

Icebreaker:
What are some factors that determine how productive or unproductive you are on any given day at work?

Segue:
When it comes to work, productivity is partly up to us and partly up to the people we work with. As a team with so many different moving parts, we're often forced to depend on others to do their jobs well so we might do ours well, too. (Share a specific example about how your staff depends on another person, position, or department in order to be excellent, and how another department depends on yours as well.)

Ask all:
If you had to nail it down to one thing, what would you say is the key to doing the very best work you can do here?

Scripture: Read John 15:1-5.

Connect & Discuss:

▶ It would never make it as a best-selling motivational book title, but Jesus said, "Apart from me, you can do nothing." For you to do the things He calls you to do, His presence and power is required. For you to grow in and through your work here, His presence and power is required.

▶ If you look at life with an eternal focus (and we should), Jesus is the foundation and Source of everything we do that really matters. Without Him, your efforts amount to....well, nothing.

▶ The good news, though, is that He wants to use you to accomplish His purposes in the world. And you can. And you should. He even tells you how to get it done. There is one and only one step to spiritual productivity—stay connected to Jesus. It's not a job that changes you. You can work here and walk away unchanged. You can (name specific things staff members do well) and still be unfruitful. It's not simply being part of what's going on here that does the changing. It's Jesus being here and working in you that does the changing.

Challenge:

Do whatever you need to remain in Him, today and every day.

Pray

Week 7

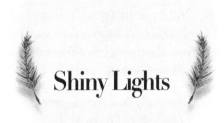

Shiny Lights

Icebreaker:

How wide would you say your circle of influence is: small, medium, or large? Why?

Segue:

Whether you have two people you think are paying attention to you or 200, (name organizational slogan or mission statement) involves you. You have something to do with who and how many people you invest in; you have nothing to do with who and how many people *they* impact as a result.

Ask all:

Name one way your work at _____ (name of organization) could impact other people, positively or negatively.

Scripture: Read Matthew 5:14-16.

Connect & Discuss:

▶ Notice Jesus says, "You are." He doesn't say, "You should be." By the very nature of being in Christ, you are the light of the world. In Him, you can't possibly *not* be.

▶ Jesus said you should let your light shine in front of people – not in an Instagram "look at my love for Jesus" sort of way, but in a live-out-your-faith-as-you-go-about-your-work sort of way. The point isn't to have influence in the world so that you get some sense of glory for yourself, but to live in such a way that Jesus influences the world and gets the glory as you let His light shine.

Challenge:

Letting your light shine involves two things: availability and obedience. We make ourselves available to shine the light when we walk with Jesus each day. We shine the light when we glorify God, moment by moment, through faithful obedience to His commands. In what way can you make yourself more available to the light of Christ as you work this week? In what way can you be more obedient to God's commands as you work this week? Shine your light; change the world.

Pray

Week 8

Team Sport

Icebreaker:

When hiring new employees, do you think we should look for people who share the same strengths and talents or who have different strengths and talents? Why?

Segue:

The business of changing the world is not for the lone wolf. The task of (name of your organization) is too important and we all have too many limitations, weaknesses, and blind spots to try to tackle it on our own. There are eternal implications to the tasks we're given here. That's why working here is a team sport. We desperately need each other.

Ask all:

Name one thing you've learned or a way you've benefitted from someone else who works here.

Scripture: Read Proverbs 27:17.

Connect & Discuss:

▶ Working as a team makes each of us better. Look around the room. We're sharper as individuals and as a group because of each other.

▶ In contrast, flying solo makes you worse. If you're not letting the team get in on the process of sharpening you, you're becoming dull. If you're not investing in the team, bringing your best to the workplace each day, you're making other people dull. [dull: adj. 1. not sharp; blunt 2. causing boredom; tedious; uninteresting. 3. not lively or spirited; listless 4. not bright, intense, or clear; dim 5. slow in motion or action; not brisk; sluggish]

▶ It's not always an easy process. When iron sharpens iron, sometimes sparks fly. But teammates intentionally encourage one another to grow, even if it involves painful criticism on occasion (See Prov. 27:6).

Challenge:

Your answer to the application question about Christ-like strengths may have helped you get the job, but living out your answer to that question will help each one of us. You are part of the team. Let's get sharp together.

Pray

Week 9

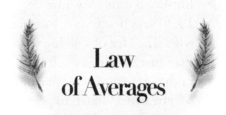

Law of Averages

Icebreaker:

Who is the wisest person you know? What about that person makes you say that?

Segue:

It has been said, "You are the average of the five people you spend the most time with" (Jim Rohn)[1]. While you can't average people quantitatively, the basic point is valid – who you spend time with influences the person you become. That can be a good thing, or that can be a bad thing.

Ask all:

Considering all of us spend at least part of our time here with our co-workers, how would you describe an average employee? Is the average employee here someone you want to become? Why or why not?

Scripture: Read Proverbs 13:20

Connect & Discuss:

▶ Jim Rohn didn't say anything new. Proverbs 13:20 says if you walk with the wise, you become wise. The idea of walking with someone is more than just hanging out. It indicates you're going in the same direction, pursuing the same goals. Maybe you're drawn to people who share your sense of humor. With them, maybe you walk in laughter. Or if you're drawn to people who are deep thinkers, you walk together in the pursuit of knowledge and truth. But within any type of personality you're drawn to, there's a choice between wisdom and foolishness.

▶ The bottom line here is that we have a responsibility to each other to pursue wisdom, whether we're at work or any other place we spend our time. Who we choose to walk with outside of this place impacts who we become inside this place. Who we are inside this place impacts who other people become outside it.

Challenge:

Be the type of person who raises everyone else's average.

Pray

Week 10

Anger Management

Icebreaker:

Play a game of word association. Name the following emotions, and direct your staff to call out their first response upon hearing each word: *happy, sad, scared, guilt, awe, worry, anger.* After ending with anger, ask, "What's the dumbest thing you've ever gotten mad about? How do you usually handle your anger: blow up, swallow it, take it out on someone uninvolved, or something else?"

Segue:

Of course, there will be times at work when your anger is stirred over someone or something. Last week we read iron sharpens iron. If we're going to do that well, we have to be careful in the way we go about it. Anger, handled poorly, can wreck a team and destroy the sharpening process.

Ask all:

Let's say you did something to make a coworker mad. How would you want that person to handle it?

Scripture: Read Proverbs 15:1

Connect & Discuss:

▶ The Hebrew word used to describe a soft or gentle answer indicates humility, not obstinacy. As the saying goes, "That'll preach!" If we're going to accomplish our God-given mission as an organization, it's going to require humility on our part. We can't respond to people in Christ-like ways if pride is our driving force.

▶ "Soft" or "gentle answer" also describes how a wound is soothed or healed. In contrast, a "harsh word" literally means "word of pain." So we have a choice. Speak with humility and bring healing, or with pride and bring pain.

▶ Don't miss what that means, practically. How you speak to other people often determines how they respond to you. This verse plainly explains that you can turn away wrath in a person, or you can stir up anger. As a staff, we can turn away wrath and bring healing in the workplace, or we can stir up anger and cause hurt.

Challenge:
We work together; we can avoid destructive factions and an "it's us vs. them" mentality through the words we choose. Whoever we're talking to, let's speak humbly and gently.

Pray

Week 11

Job Description

Icebreaker:

What task in your job description brings you the most joy? What task in your job description do you wish you could avoid?

Segue:

It's part of almost every job – stuff you like, and stuff you wish you could pass off to someone else. But whatever we are assigned, we should seek to do it well. There is purpose even in the tasks we find difficult, unpleasant, or time consuming. And, truth be told, in all tasks, we can find the greater purpose if we're looking.

Ask all:

What would you say is your greatest purpose in life? How well are you accomplishing that purpose right now?

Scripture: Read Acts 1:8.

Connect & Discuss:

▶ Jesus was about to ascend to heaven and leave the disciples He'd been molding and teaching for three years. And in leaving them, He gave them great purpose. They would be His witnesses. What happened right there in Jerusalem would change the world.

▶ But He wasn't leaving them alone. His Spirit would come upon and reside within those who would trust and follow Christ. He would fill each one of them with the very power of God to accomplish His purposes in the world.

▶ This isn't just the story of the disciples in Acts. It's the story of every person who trusts and follows Jesus. You have been given great purpose; you are God's witness in the world. It's the most important job description you'll ever receive. You are God's witnesses at (name of organization) and every other place you find yourself. He hasn't left you alone, either. His Spirit dwells in you to empower you to accomplish the task He has set before you.

Challenge:

As you do your work here, remember you don't just represent (name of organization). You are Christ's witness to the world. Witness well.

Pray

Week 12

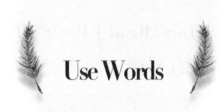

Use Words

Icebreaker:

Auditory learners learn by hearing and listening. Visual learners learn by reading or seeing pictures. Kinesthetic (tactile) learners learn by touching and doing. Which type of learner are you: visual, auditory, or kinesthetic?

Segue:

You've probably heard the quote, "Preach the gospel at all times. If necessary, use words." It is usually attributed to St. Francis of Assisi. There are a couple of problems with it, though. For one, he never said it. The closest thing to this quote in any of his writings was a statement on how Franciscan friars should practice their preaching. He wrote, "No brother should preach contrary to the form and regulations of the holy Church…All the Friars…should preach by their deeds."[2] Essentially, he was saying, "Make sure your deeds match your words," but he was never saying you don't need to preach the gospel. And this is exactly the second problem with the way the quote is often used today. *You can't preach the gospel without words.*

Ask all:

How are all three learning styles (hearing, seeing, doing) emphasized in Jesus' life and teachings?

Scripture: Read 1 Peter 3:15.

Connect & Discuss:

▶ The bottom line is this: people can't know why you live the way you live unless you tell them about Jesus. Being a positive person with morals isn't evangelism. No one can avoid hell simply because they go to church or make good choices on a Friday night. That only happens when we decide to trust and follow Jesus.

▶ Don't be mad if you were planning to make that "If necessary, use words" quote your next tattoo. Living out your faith by example can be a powerful evangelistic tool, if you remember there's more to it than that. We spread the gospel not one way, but three: through ongoing lifestyle (visual), daily actions (kinesthetic), *and speaking* (auditory).

*Since he was a friar, you might think Francis of Assisi was quiet and walked around humming Gregorian chants. But Francis was fiery, sometimes preaching in up to five villages a day using boxes as his platform and becoming so animated he almost looked like he was dancing. The point isn't that you have to be a preacher; it's that the gospel compels us to tell others what Jesus has done in our lives.

Challenge:

The crucified and risen Christ is the reason (name of organization) exists. Don't just wear the shirt. Tell somebody.

Pray

Week 13

Exposed

Icebreaker:

Have you ever felt in your heart that you were supposed to pursue a certain course of action, only to find out later you were wrong? What happened?

Segue:

Relationships are an easy example. Many of us have at one time or another believed a romantic relationship would last, only to later discover we were wrong about that. Opportunities serve as another example. We might feel in our hearts we are supposed to go on a specific trip, get a particular job, have a certain life, or even live in a particular place. But it doesn't always work out the way we believed it would, and we're left confused.

Ask all:

If you had to pick one word to describe your heart, what word would you choose? Why?

Scripture: Read Jeremiah 17:9-10

Connect & Discuss:

▶ This is God talking through Jeremiah…not to pagans, but to His people. God describes the heart with words like "deceitful" and "desperately sick." This is why saying, "I'll know in my heart what to do" or "My heart is telling me to…" is unreliable logic for decision-making. Because of its deceitfulness and desperately sick state, we are incapable of fully understanding our hearts.

▶ We can't understand the human heart, but God can. He searches our hearts and knows exactly what is in them. Our hearts are completely exposed before Him. While that might seem like really bad news, if we give our hearts over to Jesus, God sees that first and foremost. He molds our hearts, making what is otherwise deceitful and desperately sick, true and eternally whole.

▶ The person God rewards is not the one who appears to do all the right things; it is the one whose heart is exposed to the Lord and is continuously shaped in prayer and by God's Word.

Challenge:

Ask, "Based on these two verses, what would you say God desires from us as we work? How do these verses speak to our tendency to simply go through the motions? Let's not just get our work done, let's get it done with the heart of Jesus."

Pray

Week 14

**Pure
and Clean**

Icebreaker:

Name something really big you have asked God to do, either in the past or at the present time.

Segue:

Lots of us pray for God to heal the people we know who are sick. On a personal level, we might go a little deeper and ask Him to give us opportunities to serve Him or help us overcome a temptation. Every kind of prayer is important and good (Phil. 4:6). Most of the time, though, our prayers reflect a focus on outward circumstances and behaviors. We don't often get to the heart of the matter.

Ask all:

Have you ever prayed for God to change a person's heart? In what way? Have you ever asked God to change your heart? Why or why not?

Scripture: Read Psalm 51:10

Connect & Discuss:

▶ In last week's devotion, we read God's words in Jeremiah 17:9-10: "The heart is deceitful above all things and desperately sick." But the psalmist lets us know the situation isn't hopeless. We should acknowledge the deceitful, desperate sickness we find inside ourselves, but there's no reason to just sit in it.

▶ The same God who understands the depth of depravity in the human heart has the power to create a new one—pure and clean.

▶ It's like one of those really big things you've prayed for God to do, only bigger. God doesn't just have the power to help you act differently; He has the power to make you *become* different. He doesn't always remove difficult situations, but He always works in us through them. Relationship with Christ isn't about changed behavior. It's about changed hearts.

Challenge:

What difficult situation, circumstance, problem, or relationship are you facing? Invite God to get to the heart of it, and pray bigger.

Pray

Week 15

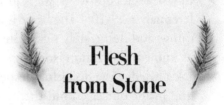

Flesh from Stone

Icebreaker:

Do you tend to cry in emotionally touching movies? If yes, what movies have driven you to tears? If no, what's the closest you've ever come to crying in a movie?

Segue:

Two people can be sitting side by side in the same movie, and one walks out dabbing tears with a tissue while the other walks out with dry eyes. Different things affect us in different ways. You may feel deeply about an issue or situation, while your coworker remains largely unconcerned. When it comes to things like movies and temporary issues at work, that's OK. When it comes to things related to God's kingdom purposes and eternity, not so much.

Ask all:

How is having a heart for God different from being an emotional person? How would you describe a person who has a heart for God?

Scripture: Read Ezekiel 11:19-20

Connect & Discuss:

- ▶ God's chosen people had divided, stony hearts.

- ▶ Their hearts had turned away from God and from His purposes for them as a nation. In exile, they were more concerned about their individual desires than about their unity and calling.

- ▶ God promised to give them a unified heart of flesh. The result? They would be a people again, a team, sensitive to God's Word and rejecting the idols that kept them from obeying it.

- ▶ Over time, hard hearts and division can develop among a people who, at their core, know and agree on who they are to be and what they are to be about. You may have experienced that here at (name of organization). But good news! God can take the hardest, most divided hearts and make them tender and whole again.

Challenge:
There were two types of people among the Israelites – those who would cling to their hard hearts, and those who would turn their hearts over to God. Every day, we get to decide which type of person we're going to be.

Pray

Week 16

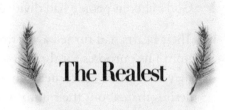

The Realest

Icebreaker:

When you're in a bad mood or are having a bad day, do the people around you usually know it? (Maybe your co-workers should answer this question for you!) What can you do to compensate on a bad day, so people don't notice?

Segue:

Everyone has bad days, where the best approach at work might be to "fake it 'til you make it." That's okay when you need to serve a group well or interact with co-workers on the job. But, spiritually speaking, it's impossible to fake it 'til you make it.

Ask all:

How would you explain what it means to be real in your faith?

Scripture: Read Matthew 5:8.

Connect & Discuss:

▶ "Pure in heart" refers to a person whose righteousness is authentic. The Pharisees faked righteousness by outward behaviors, just like people can fake righteousness with good works today.

▶ True purity of heart is given to the person who grieves not a bad day or a bad circumstance, but his or her spiritually bankrupt condition, and hungers and thirsts for God's righteousness in personal relationship with Christ.

▶ Thinking about the big picture, what does it mean that the pure in heart will "see God"? Could it also be true about a person's life on earth? Explain. If purity of the human heart is God-given (and it is!), then what, if anything, is the human responsibility in this blessing and promise?

Challenge:
Good day, bad day, or in between – seek realness in relationship with Christ and be blessed.

Pray

Week 17

No Filter

Icebreaker:

What book have you read that impacted you? How?

Segue:

Humor, relatable illustrations, motivation, fresh insights, and self-help. These are the makings of many of today's best-sellers. For the most part, we like tips for self-improvement and authors who leave us feeling good – an easy read.

Ask all:

Would you describe the Bible as an "easy read"? Why or why not?

Scripture: Read Hebrews 4:12; James 1:23-25; Jeremiah 23:29; and Psalm 119:105.

Connect & Discuss:

▶ How is the Bible described here? What is it able to do?

▶ The Bible is like the sharpest sword. And a mirror. And a hammer. And an LED lamp. This is where it gets a bit uncomfortable. We want the Bible to be like a selfie, using filters and crop tools to ignore the imperfections and make us feel good about ourselves. But the Word of God doesn't work like that. The Bible shows us who we are and where we need to make changes (Heb. 4:12 and James 1:23-25), penetrates and judges the heart (Heb. 4:12), breaks apart the hard places of our hearts (Jer. 23:29), and illuminates the way we should go (Ps. 119:105).

▶ Each of those actions then demand a response. For heart change to take place, we must not only hear God's Word, but persevere in it and do the works this sword, mirror, hammer, and lamp reveal.

Challenge:

Dig into God's Word, unfiltered, and invite Him to break apart the hard places and bring the changes He desires.

Pray

Week 18

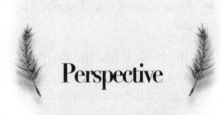

Perspective

Icebreaker:

Are you a person who worries a lot? What are some things you tend to worry about?

Segue:

It's easy to say, "Don't worry." It's much harder to keep yourself from worrying. It is an honor to be given more responsibility, but with more responsibility often comes more worry. Besides that, worry is often the very thing that drives us to take on responsibilities, like getting a job. We worry we won't have the money we need if we don't work!

Ask all:

How has your relationship with Christ helped you deal with your worries? Give specific examples.

Scripture: Read Luke 12:31-34

Connect & Discuss:

▶ The "But seek His kingdom" in verse 31 points back to the "Don't worry" in verse 22. When our focus is on God's everlasting kingdom, the temporary stuff of earth takes a backseat.

▶ Practically speaking, what does it mean to seek God's kingdom?

▶ It's a matter of focus and priority. If we let God's purposes be our focus and priority, it frees us up. We become less worried about material things and earthly success, and more concerned about carrying out His will in the world.

▶ To make God's kingdom our focus and priority, we must treasure Christ more than we value any other thing. Your perspective on life (and work!) will be determined by what you value the most.

Challenge:

Think back again to the things you tend to worry about. Turn your heart to God's kingdom priorities and let Him put those worries in perspective of eternity.

Pray

Week 19

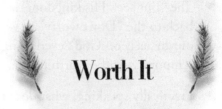

Worth It

Icebreaker:

What would you do if it meant earning a paid day off? A paid week off? Would you (name an unpleasant task at your workplace)? Would you (name a more unpleasant task at your workplace)? Would you (name one more really unpleasant task at your workplace)? Would what you'd gain be worth the price you had to pay?

Segue:

We live by a mentality of cost vs. reward. "What's in it for me?" or "Is this what I really want to do?" are the driving forces behind many of our decisions. In other words, what's it worth to you?

Ask all:

What is something you've done or given up because of your relationship with Christ? Was it worth it? How?

Scripture: Read Matthew 16:26.

Connect & Discuss:

▶ Jesus' two questions in this verse weren't like our icebreakers from today. He was talking to His disciples, and the questions were rhetorical. The answers were obvious, especially considering He'd just said if you try to hang on to your life you'll lose it, and if you give up your life for Him, you'll save it.

▶ Jesus presents the two choices as an either/or proposition. You can't chase after stuff and Jesus at the same time. You can't have the world and save your soul, too.

▶ There is absolutely no gain if a person wastes his life on himself. The rewards the world offers amount to nothing, and pursuing them means sacrificing abundant life now and full reward in eternity (v. 27).

Challenge:

Think about what it would look like for you to "gain the world but lose your soul" at work. In terms of your job, what would it look like for you to chase after Jesus, instead? It's worth it!

Pray

Week 20

Restored

Icebreaker:

When you're bummed, what do you usually do to feel better? Eat comfort food, retail therapy, talk to a friend or hang out, exercise, Netflix binge, sleep, other?

Segue:

On the days when we feel dry and lifeless, some of us want to keep moving and some of us want to sit in it for a while. But at the end of the day, a dry and lifeless soul is still dry and lifeless, even if you're with a friend about to fall asleep with a full belly while watching season 3 of your favorite show after a run in your new shoes.

Ask all:

What are some religious activities people wrongly think can remedy a lifeless soul?

Scripture: Read Lamentations 1:16 and Psalm 23:3.

Connect & Discuss:

▶ In Lamentations 1:16, Jeremiah mourns for dry and lifeless Israel, whose enemy had prevailed. Jeremiah finds no comfort for this grief in his soul.

▶ In both Lamentations and Psalm 23:3, there is no we, us, or they. There is only I, me, and my. It's personal. The grief is felt personally and restoration is given personally, too.

▶ At your lowest point, God restores your soul. When you are dry and lifeless, God brings you comfort (23:4).

▶ How would you explain to another person how he or she can experience God's restoration and comfort when life seems hopeless?

Challenge:
It's not your circumstances that can bring the change your soul longs for. Let God take what is dry and weary and bring new life.

Pray

Week 21

Never Abandoned

Icebreaker:

Name a place you wouldn't mind being left completely alone for a week. Name a place you would be terrified being left completely alone for a week.

Segue:

It's all in the location, location, location! With cell phones and technology these days, you have to work pretty hard to ever be left alone. Still, you can drop your phone in the toilet or find yourself in a remote wifi-less location or an EMP could shut down all communications.

Ask all:

What's the longest period of time you think you could endure going without your cell phone and all other forms of Internet connectivity? Why?

Scripture: Read Acts 2:25-28

Connect & Discuss:

▶ For the psalmist David, the Lord's presence continually before Him was all the connection and comfort he needed in the world.

▶ He did not fear being alone or abandoned; God would never let that happen. David's soul was eternally secure.

▶ Not only that, but David's soul was secure in the world, too, because God had made known to him the paths of life. No matter what was going on in the world around him, whether surrounded by friends, enemies, or all alone, David's soul would be glad because the Lord was with him always.

▶ In Christ, we are never abandoned or alone. We are forever connected to God's presence. How does that encourage you right now? How does it encourage you about your future?

Challenge:

God's continual, abiding presence in our lives doesn't just give us hope for eternity; it should also impact the way we live. On your best day and on your worst day; when you are at work and when you are at home; when you are surrounded by people and when you are all alone...He is with you.

Pray

Week 22

This is War

Icebreaker:

If you **had** to go *mano a mano* in battle, would you prefer it to happen by way of giant bubble ball, boxing ring, mixed martial arts, or sumo wrestling? Why?

Segue:

Most of us try to avoid activities that invite injury. Even the most competitive among us who engage in competitions such as these know when it's time to "tap out." Self-preservation eventually trumps any rush we might get from participating in battle.

Ask all:

Have you ever felt like you were in a spiritual battle? What happened?

Scripture: Read 1 Peter 2:11

Connect & Discuss:

▶ Peter's original audience was likely Gentile Christians who, because of religious persecution, had been scattered throughout Rome. Peter wrote to encourage these who were now living as "temporary residents and foreigners" to stand firm in faith.

▶ Here, Peter identifies a battle that didn't come from outside persecution or from living in a strange place. This battle comes from within every believer. The worldly passions of our own flesh wage war against our very souls.

▶ What is Peter's instruction to you regarding this battle you face every day you live on earth? Tap out! Not in the sense that you disengage from the world. That wouldn't mesh with Jesus's call to be salt and light. But He expects us to do whatever is necessary to steer clear of the temptations that threaten to take you down. Don't get in a bubble ball and try to knock Satan out with your human strength and willpower. Don't get in the ring and think you can come out victorious against Satan. Peter said to keep away.

Challenge:

Think of specific areas where you allow temptation into your life. Based on 1 Peter 2:11, what is God telling you to do?

Pray

Week 23

Why?

Icebreaker:

What is something about working here, the people who come here, or about (name of organization) in general that may be confusing to you? (Ex. Why don't we have a waffle bar waiting for us each morning? Why don't we sit in massage chairs while we work at our desks? Why does Employee X always get the cushy jobs?)

Segue:

Many "why" questions seem unanswerable. That happens on a personal level, too.

Ask all:

Is there something about you (or something you do) that others may think is weird and doesn't make sense? (Ex. eat the same exact thing for lunch every day; obsessed with growing that goatee...)

Scripture: Read Psalm 43:5.

Connect & Discuss:

▶ The psalmist was downcast and disturbed. Verses 1-2 let us know why – deceitful and wicked people seemed to have the upper hand in his life.

▶ Considering he had identified a legitimate cause, why was he so confused about being depressed? (Hint: see 5b.)

▶ The NIV asks: "Why, my soul, are you downcast? Why so disturbed within me?" Have you ever felt that way – downcast in your soul?

▶ Hope, God, praise, Savior. These are the key words in 5b that help us know how an otherwise downcast soul can change to one of joy. We put our hope in God, not our circumstance. We recognize God is God. We're not in charge and neither are the wicked people who may temporarily seem to be in charge. We praise God, no matter what, because even though our circumstances change, He never ever does. And we have a Savior who has made our future secure.

Challenge:

Think of a situation that is currently confusing or disappointing to you. Praise God in it, and invite Him to bring joy to your soul.

Pray

Week 24

A Time to Delight

Icebreaker:

Are you easily excited or do you operate on an even keel? When was the last time those around you knew you were happy?

Segue:

Like Solomon wrote, there's a time to laugh and a time to cry, right? But certain truths stick with you through all of it. Those are the things by which all your emotions – highs, lows, and everything in between – flow.

Ask all:

If you had to identify one truth that defines you above everything else, what would you say it was?

Scripture: Read Isaiah 61:10

Connect & Discuss:

▶ Isaiah didn't have a fun job. He was God's prophet, called to confront earthly kings and the nation of Israel about their sin. The whole first 39 chapters of Isaiah focus on sin, repentance, and judgment. The emphasis in chapters 40-66 are hope and restoration.

▶ For what reason did Isaiah delight? Excluding singing much-loved worship songs, what does it look like for a person to delight in the Lord? What enduring reason do you have for your soul to rejoice in God?

▶ It's only when we grasp chapters 1-39 that we respond like Isaiah did in chapter 61, verse 10. Without God, life is futile. Our sin and the judgment on that sin are impossible for us to remedy on our own. But in turning to Christ who covers us with His righteousness, we receive salvation.

Challenge:

Delight yourself greatly in the Lord today, and rejoice in God!

Pray

Week 25

Motivate

Icebreaker:

What are your top three motivators for doing an awesome job at work?

Segue:

Beyond "paycheck" and all its synonyms, we find motivation to work well in a variety of places. Usually, the people we work for and with have at least a little bit to do with it. For example, when a supervisor cuts corners, you might think "that's the way we roll around here." When a coworker slacks off and expects you to handle the bulk of the workload, you might quickly lose motivation to work hard.

Ask all:

Name someone whose work ethic motivates you to approach your own work with excellence. Explain.

Scripture: Read Hebrews 10:24-25.

Connect & Discuss:

▶ It's not just work where we help motivate each other to persevere with excellence. Think about the people whose faith has motivated you to pursue deeper relationship with Christ and more committed obedience to Him.

▶ The writer of Hebrews said, "Let us consider how we may spur one another on toward love and good deeds." What reason does he give for us to set this as a priority?

▶ It's a big deal! We should need no other motivation than this: what we do here has eternal implications, and eternity gets closer and closer every day. As that day approaches, we can know this - we'll be a better staff, better at our jobs, and better at changing the world when we commit to be a better community of believers.

Challenge:
What are ways we can spur one another on toward love and good deeds?

Pray

Week 26

Hopefully Devoted

Icebreaker:

What is one interesting fact your coworkers don't know about you?

Segue:

Among us, there are different backgrounds, experiences, personalities, and interests. It's amazing how a diverse group of people can come together and form a team.

Ask all:

Which better defines us as a group: where we've been or where we're headed? Why?

Scripture: Read Acts 2:42-47.

Connect & Discuss:

▶ 3,000 people. One day the church was about 120 people (1:15). The next, it numbered in the thousands. All of them from different backgrounds, experiences, personalities, interests, and many were even speaking different languages.

▶ Who they'd been and where they'd been wasn't the basis for community among them. It was all about who they had become, and where they were now headed.

▶ As a result, they became devoted – to God's Word, to each other, to remembering and keeping Jesus at the forefront, and to prayer. It was a covenant community – not a hobby, not a fad, not an "I'll check it out and see how I like it" kind of an attitude. It was an all-in, open heart, open hands commitment.

▶ If you're involved in a church, you've probably been taught Acts 2 principles as an important part of healthy church life. But it doesn't only apply at church; it applies anywhere Christians (Christ's Church) are together.

Challenge:

Think on this: Is your level of devotion to your co-workers based on unity in Christ, or the fact that you clock in at the same place? How does your answer affect your work community?

Pray

Week 27

Non Solo

Icebreaker:

For each of the following scenarios, would you rather be alone or with friends? Your boyfriend/girlfriend just broke up with you. You're bored. It's your birthday. You just got off work. You need to make a big decision. You just got the best news of your life. You just got the worst news of your life.

Segue:

Obviously, being alone isn't inherently a bad thing. But it can be. When we withdraw from community for an extended time, when we try to do everything on our own, when we are in trouble, when we think we don't need people – this is when isolation becomes a problem.

Ask all:

What situation or task at work requires other people's help to do well?

Scripture: Read Ecclesiastes 4:9-12

Connect & Discuss:

▶ This passage describes biblical friendship and community. This is one area of life Ecclesiastes never calls "futile."

▶ Loneliness is a theme of Ecclesiastes 4. The chapter begins with the loneliness from the oppression of life. It moves to the loneliness in toil and pursuing wealth, and then moves to the benefits of community. In biblical community, we help each other get work done, sustain and comfort each other in times of difficulty and disaster, and protect one another from enemies.

▶ There is strength in numbers. This isn't only true in a physical sense, like when we need to pull a heavy object out of the storage closet. It is also true that we find inner strength as we stand with others through temptation and the difficult circumstances of life.

Challenge:

What a great gift we have, working at a gospel-centered organization. Here, there should be built-in biblical community. Let's not take it for granted. Let's avoid the futility and loneliness of isolation by engaging with each other to be a strong cord of many strands.

Pray

Week 28

We're Good

Icebreaker:

Name one thing someone else in the room does well.

Segue:

Thinking about others' strengths doesn't come naturally. It's not typically learned, either. From the time we're little, we hear people telling us how we're the best on the team or how so-and-so shouldn't be playing ahead of us at first base. In high school, we start building our résumé for college applications. Even when we interview for a job like this one, we're encouraged to prove how we stand out above everyone else.

Ask all:

What's the danger in this type of thinking?

Scripture: Read Romans 12:3-6a

Connect & Discuss:

▶ It can be said that thinking of yourself – the things you need, the things you want, the things you're good at – is thinking of yourself more highly than you should. It's not that you don't matter; it's that everyone else does, too.

▶ Paul warned the Roman Christians (and us) not to think too much about ourselves. He said we should honestly evaluate ourselves, and then launched into his one body/many parts illustration. How does honest personal evaluation relate to being one part of the body of Christ? The recognition that you need other people's gifts and strengths just as much as they need yours.

▶ Paul went so far as to say, "We all belong to each other" (NLT).

Challenge:

It's not easy to change a lifetime habit of thinking about yourself first and foremost, especially one that will continue to be fed by the world around you. But here's a start. Make it a point to notice and compliment the strengths and gifts of your coworkers this week.

Pray

Week 29

All Together

Icebreaker:

Have you ever taken a spiritual gifts test? Of the following spiritual gifts, what would you think you would score high on: leadership, wisdom, discernment, exhortation, evangelism, service/helps, mercy, giving, hospitality? Which ones would you score low on?

Segue:

If you don't have the spiritual gift of evangelism, does that mean God doesn't hold you responsible for sharing the gospel? Obviously not (Matthew 28:19)! If you don't have the gift of giving, does that mean you shouldn't give? Nope (1 John 3:17). Just because you don't have a supernatural spiritual gift in one of these areas, it doesn't mean God doesn't expect you to demonstrate that Christ-like trait. Communicating the urgency of living out God's call on our lives (exhortation) isn't just the job of a pastor; we all must encourage each other.

Ask all:

In your own words, what does it mean to be part of the body of Christ?

Scripture: Read 1 Corinthians 12:25-27

Connect & Discuss:

▶ There it is again. Mercy isn't just the job of those who are gifted that way; it is the job of every believer. We should have the same care for each other, and if one suffers, we should all feel it.

▶ God designed His body, the church, as one unit with individual members. Kind of like our staff here at (name of your organization.)

▶ For the sake of organization and better productivity, we divide ourselves into different areas or departments. That's not the kind of division Paul describes here. "No division in the body" (v. 25) means we should never divide over non-essential issues. We should care about the same essential matters. For us here at (name of organization), what would you say are the essential matters we should all be unified about?

Challenge:

Groups splinter and fracture all the time over stuff that, in the long run, really doesn't matter that much. Let's guard the trust we've been given, having the same care for each other and for the things that matter most.

Pray

Week 30

Let It Go

Icebreaker:

If you have a complaint against a coworker, what should you do?

Segue:

There are those who shy away from any type of confrontation, and there are those who seem to thrive on it. Regardless of where you fall in the conflict continuum, every one of us can (and should) take steps toward resolution. Here at work, we've built in a system for doing that. Still, both at work and in life, the Bible gives important help on the topic.

Ask all:

How do you know when to let something go, and when you need to address it? If you're going to let it go, what does that mean?

Scripture: Read Colossians 3:12-14.

Connect & Discuss:

▶ Verse 12 begins with a reminder about who we are in Christ. When we know we are chosen by God and holy and beloved to Him, it changes the way we think about things; in particular, it changes the way we think about how we should react.

▶ The Greek word that translates as "bearing" (ESV) in verse 13 means "putting up with."

▶ "Heartfelt compassion, kindness, humility, gentleness, and patience," "just as the Lord has forgiven you, so you must also forgive," and "above all, put on love" show us that "putting up with" is not like "smh" or an eye roll emoji. It means we're supposed to endure offenses with grace, knowing that we all struggle with our sin nature.

Challenge:
Let it go.

Pray

Week 31

Nothing Wasted

Icebreaker:

What is your favorite season of the year? Why?

Segue:

Even though we might like one of the seasons best and wish it would last forever, we need all four seasons. Without the earth's tilt on its axis causing seasons, there would be no cropping pattern (so no need for that pizza oven because there would be no wheat), the whole population of earth would concentrate around the equator (places nearer to the poles wouldn't be habitable), we'd be plagued by disease (nasty stuff thrives in warm, humid climates), and our life expectancy would go way down.

Ask all:

What would you say has been the favorite season of your life so far? Most difficult? Is there a season of life you're looking forward to that you haven't experienced yet? If so, what is it?

Scripture: Read Ecclesiastes 3:1.

Connect & Discuss:

▶ God has a purpose for every season of your life.

▶ What that means, practically, is that God has a purpose for you being employed here. For however long you work at (name of organization), there is important meaning for it. Every day you come in to work, there is purpose. Every relationship formed has meaning. Every task given has significance.

▶ Solomon (the wisest dude ever) came to this conclusion while pondering life: apart from relationship with God, everything is meaningless in comparison. He realized that work is futile if it's just to earn a paycheck (2:18-26). Fun, pleasure, and laughter have no enduring qualities (2:1-2). Wealth and material things are vain pursuits (5:10). Even wise and knowledgeable men end the same way foolish men do (2:14-16). But when God is at the center of a person's life, every moment has great purpose and meaning (3:11).

▶ When your heart is set on the Lord, nothing is wasted. Not one moment.

Challenge:

No matter what season you find yourself in right now, set your heart on the Lord and know there is purpose.

Pray

Week 32

Biographical Sketch

Icebreaker:

Do you know the meaning of your name? What is it, or why did your parents give you that name? Do you have any nicknames? How did those come about?

Segue:

Where nicknames tend to reflect traits, experiences, or personality, our birth names tend to reflect who our parents desired or perceived us to be. You can live up to your given name or not. Either way, your name serves to identify you.

Ask all:

Has a parent or other family member ever told you to "Remember who you are"? What do people mean by that?

Scripture: Read 1 Peter 2:9.

Connect & Discuss:

▶ Because they had been persecuted and scattered, Peter's original audience needed to remember who they were. It didn't matter where they lived, what people called them, or how they were treated. Their identity in Christ would not change.

▶ *A chosen race* – we don't earn it or deserve it, but in our sinful state God chooses us to be His children. Our identity isn't defined by color or culture; it's defined by being chosen. *A royal priesthood.* We're not onlookers. We're active worship participants, drawing near to God with spiritual sacrifices. *A holy nation.* We're set apart for God and, because He's holy, now holiness is part of our identity, too. *A people for His possession.* We're the ones God plans to live with for eternity.

▶ These names don't just identify you (although, in and of itself, that part is pretty amazing). These names are meant to have an effect. In other words, your identity in Christ changes your life's purpose – "so that you may proclaim the praises of the One who called you out of darkness into His marvelous light."

Challenge:
Remember who you are.

Pray

Week 33

For Good

Icebreaker:

What's the hardest day you've ever had at work? What happened?

Segue:

To get the job done, you often have to do hard things. Like when (name specific examples from your work situation). We endure the difficult process because doing so demonstrates we are who we say we are as an organization.

Ask all:

What else in life is so important to you that you would operate under a "by any means necessary" mentality?

Scripture: Read Romans 8:28-29.

Connect & Discuss:

▶ You're probably familiar with verse 28. Many people think about verse 28 without also considering verse 29, too. If we do that, we can miss the point.

▶ The "good" God is working all things together for in your life is defined in verse 29. It's not to make you rich or to help you marry someone really good-looking. Simply put, His aim is to make you more like Jesus. So when you think about it all together like that, it means that if you're a believer, God will use any means necessary for spiritual growth to take place in your life. It's that important to Him.

▶ This doesn't necessarily mean that God makes bad things happen in your life so that you will become more like Jesus. It does mean He's not opposed to allowing any circumstance in your life that He can use to shape you. Your comfort and earthly success is not His priority; your conforming to the image of His Son is. In Christ, your good and His glory are one and the same.

Challenge:

Think about the hard stuff in your life you wish had never happened. Thank God for using it for your good.

Pray

Week 34

To Do

Icebreaker:

Are you the type of person who likes to make or receive a written to-do list at work so that you can cross items off when they are complete? Why or why not?

Segue:

Even if you don't make a daily to-do list, you probably have at least a mental idea of what you need to accomplish. You were hired to do certain tasks – some of those tasks remain constant and others fluctuate as situations and circumstances arise.

Ask all:

What is one task you do almost every day you are at work? Describe a time when a sudden, immediate need fell under your area of responsibility.

Scripture: Read Ephesians 2:10.

Connect & Discuss:

▶ We were created to do good works. God planned those good works in advance. Not in a to-do list kind of way. The Christian life is far too abundant and free to be relegated to crossing items off a piece of paper. But God does set situations, people, and circumstances in our path through which He desires us to do good works. He gives us gifts and abilities He intends for us to use to bring Him glory. He fills us with passions out of which He plans for us to affect change in the world.

▶ With all of those in mind, what are specific action steps you know God has purposed for you to do today?

Challenge:
"We are His workmanship, created in Christ Jesus for good works, which God prepared beforehand, that we should walk in them." Let's get going.

Pray

Week 35

It's Not About You

Icebreaker:

If you could sum up your life in one word, what would it be? Explain.

Segue:

It's not hard to think about ourselves. Our worlds tend to revolve around us. Our default setting is "me." Think about it: how many times have you already used the words "I", "me", or "my" today? There is probably at least one personal anecdote, circumstance, or worry that has been your headliner in thought and conversation already today. On at least some level, all of us think of ourselves as primary.

Ask all:

Is that a good thing or a bad thing? Is it even possible to be any other way?

Scripture: Read Romans 11:36

Connect & Discuss:

▶ In your own words, what is Paul saying?

▶ The NLT puts it this way: "For everything comes from Him and exists by His power and is intended for His glory. All glory to Him forever!" It's not about you.

▶ This is God's story; it's not yours and it's not mine. We're part of the story, but it's not about us. The danger in thinking it's all about us is that we begin to believe God cares more about our earthly comfort, success, and desires than He does in His glory and the salvation of all people. He doesn't.

▶ When we understand it's all about Him, it redefines our purpose and perspective. We, too, begin to care more about God's glory and the salvation of all people than we do our own earthly stuff.

Challenge:

Every time you find your thoughts landing on yourself today – your responsibilities, your stress, your worries, your desires – repeat Romans 11:36, and give God glory.

Pray

Week 36

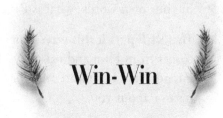

Win-Win

Icebreaker:

Are you typically a glass is half-empty person or is your glass half-full?

Segue:

Perspective is a powerful thing. It shapes our attitudes and actions. It determines the direction our lives take. When we find ourselves in difficult circumstances, perspective either prompts or prevents our worship.

Ask all:

In what situation in your life do you need a fresh perspective? How do you go about getting new perspective when you need it?

Scripture: Read Philippians 1:21

Connect & Discuss:

▶ Paul wrote these words from prison. He wasn't having a Solomon-like deep pondering about where to find the meaning of life. He had already concluded that Jesus is everything.

▶ Paul's optimism wasn't without good reason; his perspective was shaped by his theology. He saw the glass not through the lens of his circumstance, but through the lens of scripture. His understanding of relationship with Christ meant that, live or die, he was in a win-win situation. There were benefits either way. Living under any circumstance meant continued opportunities to bear fruit and bring glory to God on earth. Dying meant being in the presence of Jesus in heaven. His glass wasn't just half-full; it was overflowing!

Challenge:

The way to gain a "to live is Christ" perspective is to chase hard after Jesus. Paul's theology shaped his perspective. What's shaping yours?

Pray

Week 37

Peace

Icebreaker:

Name a news event that troubled your heart deeply.

Segue:

This devotion was written in 2016, the day after twelve police officers were shot and five were killed by snipers in downtown Dallas. Whether you read it on social media or watch it unfold on TV, the news reported around the world is rarely uplifting. Even in America, what once was believed to be a land destined for greatness is a land that seems more likely destined for destruction.

Ask all:

Does destiny change based on decision and circumstance, or is it something over which we have no control?

Scripture: John 16:33

Connect & Discuss:

▶ Jesus said these words to His disciples just before heading to the Garden of Gethsemane where He would be betrayed and arrested.

▶ The disciples would face many troubles and fears in the world. But their destiny in Christ wasn't fear; their destiny was peace. The destiny of the world is trouble; the destiny of Christ-followers is to overcome that trouble.

▶ Trouble in the world is unconditional. It plagues every one of us. Inner peace is conditional. It can only come through Jesus. Fear turns to peace when we rest our hearts and minds in the One who overcame the world.

Challenge:
Apply Jesus's overcoming victory in your life today. Live with peace.

Pray

Week 38

Glory

Icebreaker:

Who is the most famous person you've met? If you were going to be famous for something, what would you want it to be?

Segue:

The expression "fifteen minutes of fame" traces back to Andy Warhol who in 1968 said, "In the future, everyone will be world-famous for fifteen minutes." Little did he know how the internet would influence our ability to be famous!

Ask all:

If you knew you were going to have your fifteen minutes of fame tomorrow, what would you do differently today? Why?

Scripture: Read Hebrews 2:5-9 and Romans 8:16-17.

Connect & Discuss

▶ Like Jesus, we are subject to suffering for a time. Like Jesus, we are heirs of God's glory. Like Jesus, our eternal destiny is to be crowned with glory and honor and authority.

▶ In Eden, God gave humans authority over all things. In the new heaven and earth, honor, glory, and authority will be restored to us through Jesus.

▶ It should change the way we live. Far better than fifteen minutes of fame, believers are guaranteed an eternity of glory as God's children and co-heirs with Christ.

Challenge:

Fame on earth or glory for eternity – choose which pursuit you will set your heart on today.

Pray

Week 39

Present

Icebreaker:

Who is a friend you don't get to see very often, but wish you could?

Segue:

We all have people we wish we could be with. The realization of the value of a person's presence grows greater when you don't get to experience it anymore.

Ask all:

On the flip side, have you ever met someone and then later wondered how you ever got along without them before?

Scripture: Read 2 Corinthians 5:6-8

Connect & Discuss:

▶ In relationship with Jesus, we experience both the longing for His presence and the wondering how we ever got along without Him before we'd turned to Him. What an amazing gift we have been given in the Holy Spirit, the very real presence of Christ in us at all times. Still, it's hard to fully understand what we're missing out on by not being in the physical presence of Jesus.

▶ Paul described our future destiny this way: at home with the Lord. Right now, we're away from the Lord in a physical sense, but one day we'll be away from our bodies instead. In that moment and forevermore, we will find ourselves in the very real presence of the Savior. Now we walk in relationship with God by faith; then we'll walk with Him in complete and unhindered sight.

Challenge:

Take courage and live to please Jesus. This is not your home.

Pray

Week 40

Absent

Icebreaker:

What's one thing you would not miss if it disappeared from the world? (Ex. Broccoli? Spiders? Soccer? Neckties?)

Segue:

Unless you're a guest at someone's house, you get to choose what you're going to eat. If you don't like soccer, you can avoid it unless someone in your family is a player or huge fan. But other things in life you're just stuck with.

Ask all:

What's the best way to deal with the stuff you wish you could be done with, but can't avoid?

Scripture: Read Revelation 21:4

Connect & Discuss:

▶ One day you will have your very last cry. You'll experience your very last sadness. You'll feel pain for the very last time.

▶ Death is going to disappear. Forever! Your destiny of being present with the Lord forever also means you have a destiny of *absence*...absence from death, mourning, pain, and tears. And no sin, either (Rev. 21:27)! It's impossible to fathom. But it's a guaranteed done deal. There will be a new order, and none of those things are invited.

Challenge:

You can't avoid death, mourning, pain, and tears. To try would be to disengage from the life God has called you to live right now. But because those hurtful things you can't avoid will disappear forever one day, you can live that life He's called you to with hope.

Pray

Week 41

Mind Blowing

Icebreaker:
"You'd have to see it to believe it." Have you ever said those words? What have you seen or experienced that absolutely blew your mind?

Segue:
You can believe something you didn't see – that's faith. If your best friend told you the craziest story you ever heard, you'd believe it. But it wouldn't be the same as if you had been there to experience it, too. Some things you can't fully understand until you see or experience it firsthand.

Ask all:
What do you have a hard time understanding about God or heaven?

Scripture: Read 1 Corinthians 2:9-10; Job 26:14; 1 Corinthians 13:12

Connect & Discuss:

▶ Paul quoted Isaiah, who said no one could imagine what God had planned for His people. The Spirit has revealed it to us now through the revelation of Jesus Christ. Still, we only know in part.

▶ Job compared our understanding of God to a small whisper. You can hear it, but just barely. That's what relationship with God is like right now – a whisper. We know enough to have faith and experience salvation, but the understanding we have now will in heaven be more like a megaphone...like, "Oh, now I hear better. THIS is God!"

▶ Paul compared it to a mirror. It's a good assumption to think that Paul didn't spend much time in front of one, and when he did it probably wasn't the same quality as the one you looked at in your bathroom this morning. Right now, we see God dimly – as dimly as our own reflection in a first century mirror. In heaven, nothing will get in the way of full comprehension. We'll see Him face to face.

Challenge:

Don't limit God with small thinking. He's bigger than you think. Your destiny is bigger than you can imagine. When you see Him face to face, it's going to blow your mind!

Pray

Week 42

Praise

Icebreaker:

What's a task, assignment, or commitment you tried to get out of, but couldn't? Have you ever given an excuse to avoid something you didn't want to do? What happened?

Segue:

Some challenges are inevitable, whether you're looking forward to them or not. Experiencing those things, then, is much better with enthusiasm than with dread.

Ask all:

Name three things you know you can count on to happen today.

Scripture: Read Philippians 2:9-11; Luke 19:40

Connect & Discuss:

▶ Your praising God with your whole heart and mind, and acknowledging Him as Lord, is inevitable. God swears by Himself it will happen (Isa. 45:23).

▶ We have opportunities to go ahead and do that now. When Jesus entered Jerusalem and the religious leaders tried to shut the people up and stop them from praising God, Jesus told them their efforts to stop it were feeble and futile. Even the rocks are smart enough to know it.

▶ What this means is that when you kneel before the Lord Jesus one day in person, it will be with either joy or regret. We make that decision right now. Your destiny is to praise Jesus as Lord. Your choice is enthusiasm or dread.

Challenge:

Prepare now for your eternal destiny – be a worship enthusiast!

Pray

Week 43

Really Shiny

Icebreaker:

Name one way or context in which each coworker on your team seems to shine.

Segue:

When we stand out, other people notice. A pat on the back isn't the only benefit, either. When we shine in the ways God intends, it lights the way for others.

Ask all:

Whose "shiny light" helped you see Jesus better?

Scripture: Read Philippians 2:14-18

Connect & Discuss:

▶ Paul poured himself into the believers in Philippi, and he wanted it to matter. He wanted it to matter so much that he was willing to personally sacrifice everything. If these believers he mentored would impact others for Christ, Paul would rejoice, even if it meant giving up his own life for the cause.

▶ For at least 43 weeks now, we've been pouring into each other, too. We're not sacrificing much to do it, but the goal is every bit as lofty as Paul's was—that we would be blameless and innocent, children of God without blemish in the midst of a crooked generation in which we shine as lights in the world, holding fast to the word of life.

Challenge:
Where in your world can you shine brighter?

Pray

Week 44

Really New

Icebreaker:

What item do you not mind buying used? What is something you always buy new and then replace before it gets too old or worn?

Segue:

If you've ever watched the MythBusters bathroom toothbrush episode, you'd probably decided you'd like a new toothbrush every single day [http://www.discovery.com/tv-shows/mythbusters/mythbusters-database/fecal-matter-on-toothbrush/]. Most of us live in houses or apartments that have already been lived in; some of us drive cars that have had a previous owner or owners; we might wear clothes someone else has worn. But some things need to be unused. Brand new.

Ask all:

What is one new thing you'd like to see here at (name of organization)?

Scripture: Read 2 Corinthians 5:17

Connect & Discuss:

▶ Why does Paul call a Christian a new creation? What new things have come?

▶ In his letters, Paul uses the phrase "in Christ" numerous times. It's not a one-time deal, either, the day you get saved. Being in Christ means you're a brand new creation, and it also means you're engaged in a continual process of newness as you are being conformed to Christ's image (Rom. 8:29). God's saving grace in our lives changes everything, and it keeps changing everything.

▶ If the only new spiritual thing you can recall in your life points back to your initial salvation experience, you're missing out.

Challenge:

Forget about the physical stuff for a second. What would (name of organization) be like if all of us lived and related to each other like we were the new creations we are?

Pray

Week 45

Really Satisfied

Icebreaker:

What is the most satisfying meal you have had lately?

Segue:

When we eat an unsatisfying meal, we usually chase it later with something else, like a late night run to In-N-Out Burger. It's the same in life. We try to get full and find satisfaction in a thousand ways.

Ask all:

Are you satisfied in life? Why or why not?

Scripture: Read John 6:35.

Connect & Discuss:

▶ The context here is important. Jesus had just fed 5,000 people with five loaves of bread and two fish. The story behind the story is that a gigantic crowd of people were there because Jesus was doing cool stuff, and they wanted to see what was next. They were interested not so much in Him as they were in what He could do for them. We know this because the next day they showed up again and Jesus called them out on it (John 6:26-27). They told Jesus the bread and fish miracle was impressive, but they wanted more. After all, Moses had provided bread every day for 40 years. It's like they were saying, "You only fed us once. That's a good start, Jesus" (v. 31).

▶ Jesus was setting them up for what He was about to teach them. It was God who sustained them for 40 years, not Moses. "I am the bread of life" is one of seven "I am" statements Jesus made, but it really wasn't about the bread. The bread was about something bigger. God satisfied His people with bread in the Old Testament; Jesus satisfies New Testament believers with Himself.

▶ Jesus isn't your meal ticket. He wants you to love Him for who He is, not for what He can give you.

Challenge:

Nothing in this world can truly satisfy you; only Jesus can. Look no further.

Pray

Week 46

Really Valuable

Icebreaker:

Have you ever stumbled across an item of exceptional value, like money on the sidewalk, a treasure in the middle of junk at a garage sale or flea market, or a vintage doll or rare baseball card in mint condition in your grandmother's attic? Have you ever looked? What were you looking for?

Segue:

As a child, you may have asked for a metal detector. It's that dream of finding an object of great value in unexpected, common places. Jesus said that's what the kingdom of heaven is like.

Ask all:

On a scale of 1 to 10, where would your friends rate you on how deeply you treasure your salvation. On what basis?

Scripture: Read Matthew 13:44.

Connect & Discuss:

▶ It's a parable, but why do you think Jesus said the man buried the treasure again after finding it? Why did he sell everything he had and buy the whole field?

▶ The kingdom of God is a priceless treasure, but it doesn't come without cost. To follow Jesus is an all or nothing proposition. In the parable, the man joyfully gave up everything to gain God's kingdom...because it was worth it.

▶ Lots of people want to have Jesus and the world, too. We want to visit the field, not give up everything so that's all we have left. We want to go there with our friends any time we want, but only if we can go with our friends to other fun fields next.

▶ It doesn't work that way (Luke 9:62). Jesus is worth everything.

Challenge:

What would your life look like if you treasured salvation so much that nothing was off-limits to God? Invite God to give you the faith and courage to embrace the cost that comes with treasuring His kingdom above all else.

Pray

Week 47

Really Follow

Icebreaker:

What would you say are the top three keys to being a good (name of organization) employee?

Segue:

What if in the interview process, you were told that to work here, you'd have to commit to communicating, appreciating, and encouraging your coworkers? And what if you really can't stand most people and you'd rather eat dirt than communicate with them or pretend to respect their dumb ideas?

Ask all:

Would you fake it and take the job, or would you turn the job down? Why?

Scripture: Read Mark 8:34.

Connect & Discuss:

▶ In Mark 8, Jesus spent time helping the disciples understand His identity, and also the identity of those who choose to follow Him. Peter rightly identified Jesus as the Messiah (v. 29), but then wrongly suggested Jesus shouldn't talk about unfavorable topics like suffering and rejection and dying (32).

▶ This is what prompted Jesus to identify 3 musts for His followers. "If anyone wants to be My follower, he must deny himself, take up his cross, and follow Me." This is a picture of wholehearted commitment and submission. Talk about change! Following Jesus means turning from our own desires and way of thinking to follow after His, even when it doesn't seem to make sense.

Challenge:

What's a tough thing following Jesus is requiring of you? How can we help each other be better followers?

Pray

Week 48

Really Run

Icebreaker:

Do you have a heritage of faith in your family, or are you the beginning of a new heritage of faith? Who are the people whose lives have taught you what it means to follow Jesus?

Segue:

A testimony is a powerful thing. When a Christian running the race well shares their faith experiences with you, it's strong encouragement for you to run well, too.

Ask all:

Regarding your walk with Christ, where do you need to be encouraged to keep going?

Scripture: Read Hebrews 12:1-2.

Connect & Discuss:

▶ "Therefore" in 12:1 points back to the list of Old Testament heroes of the faith in chapter 11. These servants of God persevered in the faith even when they did not personally experience the fulfillment of God's promises in Christ. A witness is someone who gives testimony. Their witness testifies to faith that endures.

▶ Since their testimony is one of enduring faith, we should also get rid of sin and whatever hinders us from enduring the race before us. Picture it. An arena full of Old Testament heroes of the faith and those since them whose faithfulness has touched your life. They are cheering you on, and Jesus is before you. Fix your eyes on Him. He is your prize.

Challenge:
Run unhindered. Run well. Run to Jesus.

Pray

Bonus
Week 1

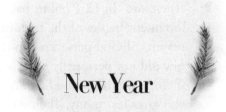

New Year

Icebreaker:

Every Major League baseball player has a "Walk Up Song" that is played in the stadium as he walks up to the plate for his turn at bat. The song is a meaningful identifier for players, and is meant to motivate him to succeed. If you had a "walk up song" to identify and motivate you as you arrive at work each day, what would it be?

Segue:

The turn of a new year is a common time for people to look for renewed identity and motivation.

Ask all:

What is something you hope to change or accomplish this year? What obstacles might keep you from it?

Scripture: Read Isaiah 40:29-31.

Connect & Discuss:

▶ In Isaiah 40, God instructed the prophet Isaiah to comfort His people. Whatever hopes they once had were no more, and they felt abandoned (See 40:27). Isaiah's message to them was to endure by placing their hope in the Lord. He renews the strength of those who feel weak and the hope of those who feel hopeless.

▶ Verses 30-31 give us two keys for success in the new year. First and foremost, we must realize we need God's strength. Age has nothing to do with it; even the most energetic and strongest among us can fail. But it isn't enough to simply acknowledge our need for God's strength, we must tap into it by placing all our hope on Him.

▶ When we do those two things, here are the promised outcomes: we will find renewed strength; we will soar on wings like eagles; we will run and not grow weary; we will walk and not faint.

Challenge:
Every day this year, no matter what circumstances you face, let Isaiah 40:29-31 be your walk up song. Find your hope and strength in the Lord.

Pray

Bonus
Week 2

Easter

Icebreaker:

Ask a few to name something they expect God to do in their lives in the coming days. Ask a few others to, in one sentence, define their mission in life. Ask the rest, "What is the primary reason you have to be joyful?"

Segue:

The message of the scriptures is that He has risen. But what does that mean, practically, in your life? What does it mean at your job? What does it mean at home?

Ask all:

Have you found practical implications the resurrection of Jesus Christ has on your daily life?

Scripture: Read Matthew 28:1-10.

Connect & Discuss:

▶ When the two Marys went to the tomb that morning, they weren't expecting anything, except to be able to carry out the duty of embalming Jesus' body with spices (Luke 24:1). The earthquake that set up the angel's arrival and announcement quickly let the two women know their low expectations were misplaced. However, the angel told them to not fear because Jesus had conquered death. The resurrection proves we should not limit our expectations of Jesus' revealed power in our lives.

▶ Not only did their expectations change, but so did their mission. In fact, Jesus showed up in person to reiterate the same mission the angel had given the women – go and tell. The resurrection frees us from a same old, same old lifestyle. We should live on mission.

▶ When the women headed to the tomb that morning, their hearts were the antonym of the joy they had in verse eight. Before they discovered that the tomb was empty and Jesus was alive, they were likely bowed down with sorrow, dread, and defeat. The resurrection means that whatever circumstances we face from now on, we have reason for joy.

Challenge:
Because of the resurrection of Jesus, you can expect more out of life, be more on mission, and know more joy.

Ask God to give you those things in greater measure than ever before.

Pray

Bonus
Week 3

Thankfulness

Icebreaker:

Invite the group to share Thanksgiving plans or traditions they look forward to sharing with family or friends. Many people say Thanksgiving is their favorite holiday. Why do you think that is?

Segue:

Giving thanks is good for the soul. And there is always something to be thankful for, even when we don't feel like it.

Ask all:

Name what you're thankful for outside of your work here. Name something you're thankful for related to your work here.

Scripture: Read Psalm 92:1-2.

Connect & Discuss:

▶ The psalmist said it is good to give thanks and declare God's lovingkindness in the morning. He also said it is good to give God thanks and declare His faithfulness at night.

▶ Before anything comes our way each day, good or bad, God is loving and kind. And at the end of each day, good or bad, God is faithful. This should impact our view of thanksgiving today and every day of the year.

▶ We tend to camp out on physical blessings—the stuff we can see and touch. But beyond those temporary, circumstantial things, God is still loving, kind, and faithful. So we can thank Him for the people in our lives, but also for the blessing of being part of the family of God that will never end (Jn. 1:12). We can thank Him for the food, but also that Jesus is the bread of life (Jn. 6:35), satisfying us eternally. We can thank Him for health, but also for the life of the Spirit in us (2 Cor. 4:16). We can thank Him for provisions, but also that He is our shelter (Ps. 46:1), clothes us with His presence (Rom. 13:14), and promises eternal possessions nothing can destroy (Matt. 6:19).

Challenge:
This week, let God broaden your understanding of what you can be thankful for.

Pray

Bonus Week 4

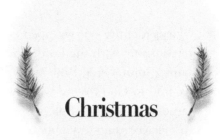

Christmas

Icebreaker:

In week 32, we discussed nicknames. Now let's go deeper. If it's appropriate, and if you feel you can trust this group not to use it against you, tell them a nickname you have been given.

Segue:

It wasn't a nickname, *per se*, but there were numerous people in scripture who self-identified as slaves or servants of God. Mary, the mother of Jesus, was one of them.

Ask all:

Relate that to today. Describe a person who could honestly pull off the nickname, "Lord's servant." What characteristics would make it true?

Scripture: Read Luke 1:38.

Connect & Discuss:

▶ Mary's identity was wrapped up in her spiritual relationship with the Lord. The same was true for James, John, Peter, Paul, and a long list of others we find in God's Word who lived their lives by the same hope Mary so boldly expressed – "Let it be to me according to your word." (See James 1:1; Rev. 1:1,9; Rom. 1:1; Phil. 1:1; 2 Cor. 5:20; Titus 1:1-3; Philemon 1:1; Jude 1:1.)

▶ These confident and unapologetic declarations of transformed identity confront us with an important truth—our understanding of who we are has a direct correlation to what we do. More personally stated, your perceived identity determines the reality of your obedience to God's call on your life.

▶ When we see ourselves as God's servants and slaves, we're compelled to obey His commands. When we identify as ambassadors for Christ and partners in the tribulation, kingdom, and endurance that are in Jesus, we look for ways to proclaim His gospel every day.

▶ Mary said, "I am the servant of the Lord." Does that statement ring true for you? We must ask: *Who do I understand myself to be? Am I operating under an identity that aligns me under God's authority, or do I ascribe authority to myself?*

Challenge:

If your identity is defined by anything other than Jesus, then carrying out your God-given purpose is impossible. This Christmas, pursue a self-awareness that is marked by submissiveness to Christ.

Pray

About the Author

Cynthia Hopkins and her husband, Clay, have served in vocational church ministry for 27 years.

Cynthia is the author of *What Now?* and she is a speaker and the writer of scores of articles, devotions, and Bible study curriculum pieces, published by LifeWay Christian Resources. She speaks regularly at women's retreats and events. You can check out her blog at cynthiahopkins.org.

Cynthia is also the marketing coordinator for Lakeview Camp and Retreat Center. She runs the website and all social media accounts, as well as helps to create and organize various youth and women's retreats and events.

Camps and retreats were a vital part of Cynthia's own spiritual development during the teenage years. Through the years, she has served as a camp attender, camp counselor, and camp/retreat coordinator. She has a heart for teenagers to know the reality of spiritual commitments in their daily lives.

Cynthia and Clay have been married for 27 years, and are the parents of two young adults: Brandon and Abby. They live in College Station, TX, where Clay serves as Associate Pastor at First Baptist Church and Cynthia teaches in the college class and helps lead women's events.

Endnotes

[1] https://www.goodreads.com/quotes/1798-you-are-the-average-of-the-five-people-you-spend

[2] http://www.ncregister.com/blog/gstanton/what-st.-francis-of-assisi-didnt-actually-say

Made in the USA
Las Vegas, NV
15 March 2023